HOW WE LIVED...

ON THE
OLD WESTERN
FRONTIER

HOW WE LIVED...
ON THE OLD WESTERN FRONTIER

by R. Conrad Stein

BENCHMARK BOOKS

MARSHALL CAVENDISH
NEW YORK

ACKNOWLEDGMENT

For his generous assistance and expert advice, the author wishes to thank
Clarence G. Seckel, Jr., Curriculum Coordinator in the Social Studies,
East Saint Louis School District 189, East Saint Louis, Illinois.

Benchmark Books
Marshall Cavendish Corporation
99 White Plains Road
Tarrytown, New York 10591-9001

• • •

Library of Congress Cataloging-in-Publication Data
Stein, R. Conrad
On the old western frontier / R. Conrad Stein
p. cm—(How we lived)
Includes bibliographical references and index.
Summary: Describes the life of the pioneers who settled the forest lands lying between
the Appalachian Mountains and the Mississippi River between 1790 and 1840.
ISBN 0-7614-0909-2 (lib.bdg.)
1. Northwest, Old—History—1775-1865—Juvenile literature. 2. Northwest, Old—Social life
and customs—Juvenile literature. 3. Frontier and pioneer life—Northwest, Old—Juvenile literature.
4. Pioneers—Northwest, Old—History—Juvenile literature. 5. Southwest,—Old—History—Juvenile literature.
6. Southwest, Old—Social life and customs—Juvenile literature. 7. Frontier and pioneer life—Southwest, Old—Juvenile literature.
8. Pioneers—Southwest, Old—History—Juvenile literature. [1. Northwest, Old. 2. Southwest, Old.
3. Frontier and pioneer life—Northwest, Old. 4. Frontier and pioneer life—Southwest, Old. 5. Pioneers.] I. Title. II. Series.
F483.S68 2000 98-23100 978—dc21 CIP AC

• • •

Printed in Hong Kong
1 3 5 6 4 2

• • •

Book Designer: Judith Turziano
Photo Researcher: Debbie Needleman

• • •

PHOTO CREDITS

Front cover: Courtesy of Lee Snider/Corbis; pages 2–3: detail St. Louis Art Museum, Ezra H. Linley Fund;
pages 6–7: Corbis-Bettmann; page 9: Washington University, St. Louis, USA/Bridgeman Art Library, London/New York;
pages 10–11, 29: The Newberry Library/Stock Montage; pages 12, 14, 18, 20–21, 23, 25, 30–31, 32, 43, 45, 46, 48, 50–51,
55, 56: North Wind Picture Archives; page 16: Museum of Fine Arts, Boston, Bequest of Henry L. Shattuck in memory of the late
Ralph W. Gray; page 26: Nancy Carter/North Wind Picture Archives; page 33: Stapleton Collection/Bridgeman Art Library,
London/New York; page 34: Private Collection/Art Resource, NY; pages 37, 40–41, 52: Stock Montage; page 38: Chicago Historical
Society, IL, USA/Bridgeman Art Library, London/New York; page 57: Minnesota Historical Society/Corbis

Contents

 A Young Nation Looks Westward

"I am listening to the tread of the coming millions!"

—HENRY CLAY, AMERICAN STATESMAN,
*upon looking west while riding alone
along the Appalachian Mountains
in the early 1800s*

There was little to do in the tiny village of Pittsburgh, Pennsylvania, in 1787. A soldier who was stationed there counted the rafts he saw floating toward the broad Ohio River. He counted fifty such rafts during the course of the year. The very next year more than one thousand rafts and flatboats streamed through Pittsburgh heading west. Aboard the vessels were farm families huddled with their pigs and cows. They were the first wave of pioneers traveling to a new land.

The United States gained its independence from Great Britain in 1783. At the time most Americans lived on a narrow strip of land that hugged the Atlantic Ocean. To the west rose the peaks of the mighty Appalachian Mountains. The mountains served as a barrier, a fence penning the people along the Atlantic shore.

But even before the Revolutionary War bands of trappers and pioneers had trekked west of the mountains. The early visitors told of a country with forests so thick the sun never reached the ground. The land there was alive with deer, bears, and a hundred other game animals. Certainly danger lurked in this untamed territory. Native Americans of the West considered the white settlers to be invaders. Still, in the young nation's mind, this wilderness loomed as the western frontier.

In American history the western frontier is more of a concept than it is a geographic area. It is a concept that changed over time. In the late 1700s the western frontier was the land lying between the Appalachian Mountains and the Mississippi River. Pioneers settled that region largely between 1790 and 1840. Later the concept of the western frontier expanded again and again until the nation reached the Pacific Ocean. This book will concentrate on the old western frontier, lands that include the present-day states of Kentucky, Tennessee, Ohio, Indiana, Michigan, Illinois, and Wisconsin.

The settlers who ventured into the frontier some two hundred years ago were a remarkable lot. Most were farm families. They were attracted to the inexpensive, fertile land the frontier had to offer. They sold their farms in the East and pushed boldly into the western forests. Their survival would depend on their ability to turn raw land into productive farms. Despite the hazards they faced, the settlers thrived. In a few short decades

DANIEL BOONE, GREATEST OF THE PATHFINDERS

In 1775 the famous explorer Daniel Boone led a party of pioneers through the Cumberland Gap in the Appalachians and into present-day Kentucky. His followers built a fort and a town called Boonesborough. Other pioneers followed Boone's path. As a result Kentucky and Tennessee were the first lands west of the Appalachians that were settled by American pioneers. Daniel Boone was a true lover of the wilderness. Even as an old man he lived in the wilds of Missouri, at the very edge of the western frontier.

Some called them foolish, others called them brave. Either way, the pioneers had to face hardship and danger. Even Daniel Boone lost his son James on his first trip leading settlers west.

they transformed the forests into communities with homes, churches, and schoolhouses. This is the people's story of the old western frontier—how the settlers lived, played, and worshiped. It is a story of triumph achieved by brave men and women.

⋙2⋘
Taming a Rugged Land

*"I was struck with astonishment; at less than 154 miles
distance from Philadelphia all trace of men's presence disappeared.
Nature, in all her primeval vigor, confronted us. [We saw]
forests as old as the world itself."*

—CHARLES MAURICE TALLEYRAND-PERIGORD,
A FRENCHMAN TRAVELING INTO THE OLD
WESTERN FRONTIER IN 1794

THE PIONEER VANGUARD

In the late 1700s mountain passes through the Appalachians were little more than foot trails. Therefore a family traveling from the East could bring only a few essential tools to the western frontier. Upon arriving they would have to live off the land. This meant making their house, their furniture, and most of their tools from whatever materials the land provided.

Every family took an ax and a rifle to the West. Also needed were a few iron cooking pots and perhaps a spinning wheel to make cloth for clothes.

As if the trail weren't rough enough, the pioneers had to struggle with the racing rivers of the frontier. Soon flatboats were a common sight, taking goods and animals across the wide Ohio River.

JOHN CHAPMAN, THE FOLK HERO CALLED JOHNNY APPLESEED

John Chapman was a flesh-and-blood man, born in Massachusetts in 1774. At about age twenty-three he wandered into the old western frontier's Ohio Valley, and there his legend began. It is said he planted apple trees in clearings. However, he never stayed in one spot long enough to reap any of the fruit. Instead he was content to let pioneers who came after him enjoy the juicy apples. Folk tales say Chapman was a religious mystic who could talk to the animals of the forest. He died in Indiana in 1845. Songs, poems, and stories were written about this curious man who later generations hailed as "Johnny Appleseed."

Most settlers brought animals—cows, pigs, and dogs. During the journey even the milk cow was fitted with a pack over her back and loaded down with goods. Settlers tried to carry a few luxury items. Treasured goods might include a clock, a violin, or any book other than the Bible. The Bible was considered to be essential.

Once on the western side of the mountains many pioneers built rafts out of logs and floated westward on the rivers. The broad Ohio River was a highway for pioneer flatboats. In 1802 a visitor near the Ohio heard an amazing chorus of cows mooing and dogs howling and wrote, "On ascending the riverbank, I perceived in [rafts] many families, carrying with them their horses, cows, poultry. . . . These people were abandoning themselves to the mercy of the stream, without knowing the place where they should stop."

Along the riverbanks rose the great American forest. So thick and widespread were the trees that pioneers delighted in telling a story about them. They claimed a squirrel could start in the Appalachians and hop from tree branch to tree branch all the way to the Mississippi River with its feet never touching the ground. The story was not entirely true. Broad prairies spread through many parts of Illinois and Indiana. But most of the old western frontier was a vast expanse of mighty oaks, beeches, sycamores, and pines. Many had trunks five feet thick. Their crowns, seeking sunlight, pierced the sky. The woodlands of the West had stood undisturbed for hundreds of years.

The journey was over, but the challenges had just begun.
Now came the hard work of carving a home out of
the wilderness. Everyone lent a hand.

THE LOG CABIN FRONTIER

Settlers traveling by river looked for level ground and a reliable source of water. They were experienced farmers with a keen eye for land. Once a family decided on a farmstead their raft was useless because it could only sail downstream. So they disassembled the craft and dragged the cut logs ashore to build a temporary house. Any nails used in the construction of the flatboat were saved. Nails and other iron objects were almost as valuable as silver on the old western frontier.

Most families arrived in the spring and planted corn crops immediately. In order to plant in thick forests, the pioneers used a practice called girdling. With an ax a farmer made a deep cut all around a tree trunk. Girdling killed the trees, so that by summertime they were leafless. Because the trees had no leaves, sunlight penetrated and nurtured the corn. As the years went by the farmer removed the trees one by one.

People traveled and settled in groups. Instant log cabin communities rose in the forests.

Erecting a snug log cabin was often a community project. All neighbors did their part in a "house-raising." Men cut logs about sixteen feet in length, hauled them to the house site, and lifted them into place. Notches were chopped near the ends so the logs locked together firmly at the corners. This was the heavy work, usually assigned to teams of men. Women and girls filled in the cracks between the logs with mud and clay. With everyone working together a house-raising was completed in about a week. Then the people celebrated by throwing a party that lasted at least a full day.

The bare ground served as cabin floor for the first year or two. Eventually the pioneer family built a floor of split logs with the flat sides turned up. The split logs were called puncheons. Some families inaugurated a new floor by scattering cornmeal over the puncheons. Doing so, they believed, would bring good fortune to the house.

The cabin door was made of logs and swung from hinges of thick leather. Window holes were cut, but glass was nonexistent in the early days

SQUATTERS AND BUYERS

The land the pioneers claimed was not free. It belonged to the United States government. The government, however, was eager to develop the western frontier. The government sold the land for as little as $1.25 an acre. The settlers had three years to pay. Problems came from squatters, people who farmed the land without paying the government. Shooting wars erupted between squatters and settlers who had legitimately bought a section of land. Even President George Washington had difficulty evicting squatters from the land he had purchased on the old western frontier.

The Squatters, *by frontier artist George Caleb Bingham. Squatters lived in constant fear that a government agent would come to evict them.*

of the western frontier. The settlers put animal hides over the windows.

The roof was covered with shingles. Some shingles were simply made, from tree bark. Others were made of wood. A pioneer would drive a wedge-shaped knife into a log with a hammer and pry out thin pieces of wood. Because nails were scarce, the shingle roof was weighted down with logs. A half dozen or so short logs, placed on each side of the slanted roof, held the shingles in place.

The settlers of the western frontier were perhaps the greatest ax-men in history. When armies of them attacked the forest the sounds of iron meeting wood raised a symphony. An English traveler named William Cobbett said of the frontiersmen, "An *ax* is their tool, and with that tool they will do *ten times* as much in a day as any other men I ever saw. Set one of these men upon a wood of timber trees, and his slaughter would astonish you."

But did the settlers ever consider conserving at least some stands of the magnificent forests? Sadly, few pioneers thought like modern conservationists. Most looked upon trees as enemies, obstacles to farming. Logs they could not use for houses or fences were rolled into heaps and burned. The fires turned nights into blazing days. As early as the 1840s

REFORESTATION

The old western frontier was stripped so bare of trees that later residents lacked shade. By the 1840s towns in southern Ohio began to plant shade trees along their streets. Locust trees were chosen because they grew quickly. At the time the locusts were planted many of the original settlers still lived in the Ohio towns. No doubt those aging ex-pioneers thought it ironic that their children had to plant shade trees on land where the forest was once so thick that people walked in the dark even at midday.

Settlers used a plumping mill to grind corn into fine piles of meal.

much of the great western forest had become a patchwork of treeless farms.

FOOD: PRODUCTS OF THE LAND

Hunting was not sport on the western frontier. In the early days it was a serious business. Deer were the prized game animals. A single deer could feed a family for many days. A skilled hunter knew that the animals had a keen sense of smell and hearing, but faulty eyesight. So the hunter stood stiff as a statue near a waterhole or a salt lick and waited for a deer to approach.

Most frontiersmen were crack shots with their rifles. They could bring down a running deer at 150 yards. Fathers taught hunting skills to their young sons. One historian of the frontier said, "Boys of twelve hung their heads in shame if detected in hitting a squirrel in any part of the body than its head."

Wild turkeys were also sought by pioneer hunters. To kill turkeys many hunters used tricks they learned from Indians. The Indians taught frontiersmen to leave a trail of corn on the forest floor. Following the trail, the turkey walked into a snare. Hunters also learned to make the gobbling sound of a female turkey in order to lure a male forward. Some hunters sounded the turkey call by blowing through a flute they fashioned from a turkey's hollow wing bone. An adult wild turkey weighed as much as twenty pounds. Its meat was savored on frontier tables.

On the western frontier, men and boys hunted while women and girls cooked, gardened, and made clothes. But this arrangement was often upset by death or illness in the family. A single woman living on the frontier had to hunt to feed her family. Often she became as skilled a hunter as any man.

Corn, wild game, and pork were mainstays of the frontier diet. A favorite dish was "hog an' hominy," meaning pork served with corn mush. Pioneers ground corn kernels into a fine powder called meal. The cornmeal was mixed with milk or water to make a porridge. Or the meal was cooked to form bread. Cornbread had various names: ashcake, johnny-cake, or corn pone. A big plate of cornbread was served at every table on the western frontier. A farmer who raised a poor corn crop was considered to be a failure by his neighbors, as the lines from this popular song indicate:

I'll sing you a song and it won't take long,
Concerning a man who wouldn't hoe corn.

3
Life on the Log Cabin Frontier

"A pair of good horses, a wagon, a cow, a couple of pigs, several domestic fowl, two plows, together with a few other tools and implements are all that is necessary for a beginning. A log house can soon be erected."

—FROM A PAMPHLET, WRITTEN ABOUT 1818, CALLED *ILLINOIS AS IT IS*. *The pamphlet advised eastern farmers how to prepare for life in the Illinois Territory of the western frontier*

THE COMFORTS OF HOME

At first, log cabin life was crude. The family slept on bearskins spread over the floor. But pioneers gradually made their homes more livable by adding beds, chairs, tables, and dishware. Children did their part in making these items, learning as they worked.

The father was generally the family carpenter. To build a bed he began by drilling holes in the log wall with a tool called an auger. He then stuck poles into the holes and attached the free ends to a notched log. In this way he created bed rails elevated above the floor. Sticks laid crosswise served as bed slats. Dry leaves or grass were stuffed into a sack and used as a mattress.

When time permitted, the father added a bedroom loft to the cabin. The loft was a simple wooden floor built just below the slanting portion of the roof. A ladder allowed family members to climb in and out of the space. It was a custom—no one knows why—for boys to sleep in the loft.

A table was created by building a slab from split logs and then attaching the slab to four log legs. This process was accomplished without nails. To hold the pieces of wood together the pioneer drilled holes and punched wooden pegs through them. Chairs were made in the same manner. Pegs were also driven into log walls and used as hooks for hanging clothes. Boys were given the job of whittling the pegs out of sticks. Many boys became expert wood-carvers. A boy skilled with a knife also learned how to fashion dinner plates and serving spoons out of raw wood.

When wind howled and snow piled up outside, the family sat around the fireplace trying to keep warm. Some sort of fire was kept glowing night and day, all summer and all winter. Matches did not appear in the West until well into the 1840s. If a fire went out, a settler had to start a new one by striking flint to steel and making sparks. This fire-starting method was painfully slow in the freezing cold. Often a child was sent to a neighbor's cabin to bring back a burning coal in a metal pan.

Despite winter's perils some settlers saw beauty in the frozen land. A woman who emigrated from England to Illinois decsribed winter nights

This frontier kitchen is a stir of activity.
Almost everything in it was made by hand.

as "at once inexpressibly cold and poetically fine. The sky is almost invariably clear and the stars shine with a brilliance entirely unknown in England. Cold as it was, I often stood at the door of our cabin, admiring their luster and listening to the wolves, whose howlings among the leafless woods at this season are almost unceasing."

WOMEN'S WORK

Mothers and daughters did the cooking, gardening, cleaning, laundry, and clothes making for the family. No one questioned the assignment of different jobs to men and women. But the arrangement meant that women had to toil over their spinning and sewing by firelight long after the men and boys went to bed.

In the summer women cooked outside over an open fire. On rainy days

COOKING WITH CORN

Corn was so valuable on the western frontier that it was used as money. A farmer who wanted to buy a shovel from a neighbor would negotiate the price in terms of bags of corn, not cash. Frontier women cooked cornbread in open skillets over a smoky fire. Here's an easy recipe that you can make in the oven.

CORNBREAD

1 cup flour
1/4 cup sugar
4 teaspoons baking powder
1 cup yellow cornmeal

2 eggs
1 cup milk
1/4 cup vegetable oil

Sift the flour, sugar, and baking powder into a mixing bowl. Stir in cornmeal, eggs, milk, and oil. Beat with an electric mixer until smooth, about 1 minute. Pour into a greased 9 inch square baking pan. Bake at 425 degrees Fahrenheit for 20 to 25 minutes. Tip: eat while still hot and top the cornbread with butter or honey.

or in the winter the family's iron pot was hung over the fireplace. Some fireplaces featured a built-in iron bar attached to a hinge. The hinged bar was a luxury item brought from the East. It allowed a woman to swing the pot in and out of the fireplace with little risk of burning her hands.

When both meat and vegetables were available the mother made a stew. She filled the kettle halfway with water, added strips of meat, and put in potatoes or turnips as the water boiled. Whenever possible she flavored the stew with salt. Salt was also used to preserve meat, so it was a precious item on the frontier. Settlers walked many miles to gather salt at a salt lick, a place where salt collected naturally on the ground.

Mothers and daughters worked together in the family vegetable garden. Potatoes, beans, turnips, and cabbages were important vegetables because they stored well. Families kept their vegetables in a root cellar, a dug-out pit covered by a wooden door. When stored in the root cellar, vegetables resisted freezing in the winter. Women gardeners grew sage, thyme, and mustard to spice up the family's bland diet. They also gathered plants that they believed had medicinal qualities. A tea made from the root of a sassafras was thought to reduce fevers.

Clothes were treasured items on the frontier. Clothing was handmade and required many hours of tedious labor. When shirts, trousers, and dresses developed tears, they were repaired with stitching and patches. Rarely was worn-out clothing discarded. Instead, clothes were handed down father to son, mother to daughter, and had years of use.

When working outside, many pioneers wore a jacket and trousers made from deer-

This turkey hunter, wearing a sturdy deerskin outfit, has had a successful day.

*Pioneer women spent hours at looms like this one,
weaving strong cloths of linen or linsey-woolsey.*

skin. When wet, the jacket became stiff and pinched the flesh painfully. No one had underwear on the frontier. In the winter deerskin clothes froze solid. Putting on a pair of frozen deerskin trousers was like putting stovepipes over one's legs. Shoes were made of animal hide, and were usually fashioned by the father. The homemade boots did not come in left and right versions: they were the same.

The frontier's most comfortable clothing was made from a crop called flax. The stems of the flax plant were first softened by soaking in water. Then, women scraped the stems of flax between two boards to free its fibers. The long stringy fibers were then dried in the sun. After drying, the fibers were spun on a spinning wheel to create yarn. The yarn was woven

THE OLD NORTHWEST TERRITORY

The frontier region that lay north of the Ohio River was called the Northwest Territory. It was pioneered largely by "Yankees" from New York and the New England states and by emigrants from northern Europe. Both groups had strong beliefs in the value of schooling for children. The territory was governed by the Northwest Ordinance, a remarkable act passed by Congress in 1787. The Northwest Ordinance declared, "Means of education shall forever be encouraged." The ordinance required sections of land to be set apart for use by future colleges and universities.

The Northwest Territory was divided into five complete states and a part of Minnesota.

into cloth. Finally the women sewed the cloth into shirts, trousers, dresses, and sunbonnets. Women also spun the wool of sheep to create yarn for clothes and blankets. A tough cloth called linsey-woolsey was made by weaving flax and wool together. Making clothes on the frontier took days and weeks of diligent work.

Homespun clothes were sturdy. Some were also handsome to look at. In 1927 a hundred-year-old woman named Harriet Connor Brown recalled her Ohio childhood and said, "My mother used to spin. She made beautiful fine thread. . . . I remember too, that my mother raised flax, spun it into linen, wove it into cloth—colored blue in the yarn—made it up into a dress for me which she embroidered in white above the hem. I wish I had kept that dress to show my children the beautiful work of their grandmother."

SCHOOL DAYS

Men and women came to the western frontier carrying one book: the Bible. Many children learned to read by following, word by word, the passages of the Bible as their parents read aloud. Yet in most log cabin villages schools were quickly established. Usually the first community buildings to be erected were a church and a schoolhouse. The schoolhouse, like the rest of the village buildings, was a one-room log cabin.

In the early days of the frontier, most teachers were male, and they were not paid for their services. Instead the teacher was "boarded out," meaning he was given free room and board by various households.

Basic subjects such as reading, spelling, and arithmetic were emphasized in the frontier schoolhouse. Paper was rare. There were no blackboards. Pupils wrote on slabs of wood, using charcoal as pencils. They read and recited lessons together. In the silence of frontier lands, group recitations from a schoolhouse could be heard half a mile away.

Classroom discipline could be severe. Some teachers kept a slender stick called a switch hanging from pegs in full view of the students. Unruly children were switched, usually on the legs. Those who were punished by the teacher did not complain to their parents. If you got

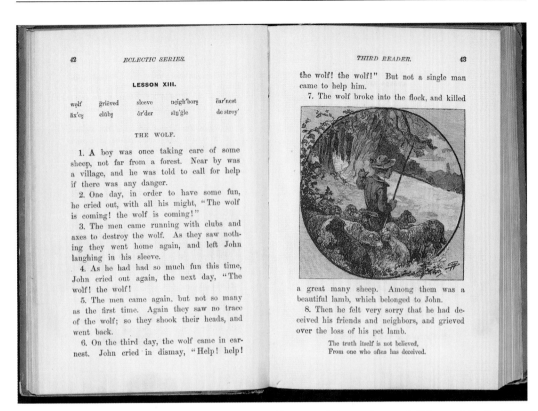

McGuffey Readers *helped educate millions of American children. McGuffey himself was a dedicated teacher, leading his first class at the age of thirteen.*

your legs switched it was your own fault.

In class as many as a dozen children shared a single textbook. The most famous of all nineteenth-century American textbooks was first published in 1836 in the frontier town of Cincinnati, Ohio. The book was compiled by a professor named William Holmes McGuffey. The *McGuffey Readers* contained passages from Shakespeare as well as speeches by American patriots. Stories in the readers had moral endings that urged boys and girls to lead upright lives. Over the years more than 120 million of these illustrated books were printed. The books were sold to schools in every part of the United States and gave millions of children their introduction to reading. In many respects *McGuffey Readers* were among the most influential American books of the 1800s. And they were first published on the western frontier.

⇛4⇚
A People
of Faith

*"A new exercise broke out among us, called the jerks,
which was overwhelming in its effect upon the bodies and
minds of the people. No matter whether they were saints
or sinners they [were] seized with a convulsive jerking
all over…. I have seen more than five hundred persons
jerking at one time in my larger congregations."*

—PETER CARTWRIGHT, A METHODIST MINISTER
WHO PREACHED IN PIONEER KENTUCKY DURING
THE EARLY 1800s

THE PASSION OF CHURCH MEETINGS

The log cabin frontier was a collection of communities. Certainly there were a few lone wolves in the West. In Kentucky and Tennessee an old saying advised a person to move "whenever you can see the chimney smoke of your neighbor." But most people, even those whose nearest neighbor was a mile away, identified themselves with a town, a

Traveling preachers called circuit riders braved all sorts of weather to bring their message of faith and hope to the settlers. One Methodist minister named Peter Cartwright traveled the frontier for fifty years and gave more than 14,000 sermons.

SLAVERY AND THE FRONTIER

The Northwest Ordinance outlawed slavery in the Northwest Territory. Slavery was legal south of the Ohio River in Kentucky and Tennessee, but few pioneers brought slaves to the land. The dividing line between slavery and freedom that existed at the Ohio River provided a dramatic setting for a famous book. In 1852 Harriet Beecher Stowe, an Ohio resident, published *Uncle Tom's Cabin*. In a gripping scene a slave named Eliza runs from Kentucky, crossing the frozen Ohio River with her baby in her arms. Chasing her are slave-catchers armed with guns. The best-selling book infuriated leaders in Southern states. In some slave states just having the book in one's home brought a jail sentence to the home owner.

Eliza's escape was a scene Harriet Beecher Stowe had witnessed many times. For eighteen years she lived across from a slave town on the Ohio River. She came to the aid of many slaves who crossed the water to freedom.

village, or a county. Nothing brought the wilderness communities more closely together than a church meeting. A deep faith in God was the foundation of the western frontier.

Early pioneers were served by brave ministers called circuit riders. Such a minister rode horseback over Indian country and through forests where there were no roads. In his saddlebags were a Bible and a few hymn-books. When he arrived at a community the words, "The preacher is here!" flashed from cabin to cabin. Everyone came to the services. The ministers preached morals and Christian behavior. They urged frontiersmen to shun

Thought to be severe in their beliefs, the Shakers actually enjoyed dancing and singing.

"corn licker," the fiery whisky made by local distillers. Some preachers, especially the Methodists, were among the first American clergymen to speak against slavery.

Before churches were built, Sunday meetings were held in a clearing. The preacher stood on a tree stump. The congregation sat on the ground. These open-air services were called camp meetings. They went on for hours. The church sessions featured singing and the passionate reciting of prayer. Some meetings were so spirited the people gave way to hysteria. Said a witness to one frontier church service, "The preachers became frantic in their exhortations.… Shouts, incoherent singing, sometimes barking as of an unreasoning beast, rent the air."

Sermons were simple, direct, and hard-hitting. A preacher kept the congregation tense by warning of death and hellfire. An Indiana pioneer remembered sermons that "struck out right and left, and rained blows on the heads of devils and bad men like fire and brimstone on Gomorrah."

An emotional high point in the services came when a man or woman stood up and "testified." A person testifying admitted to leading a sinful life, but as of that moment denounced sin forever. Sometimes young men who came to the meetings only to flirt with young women got caught up in the frenzy. A sinful young man was called a hard bat on the frontier. When a hard bat promised to sin no more, his testimony was greeted with excited cries of "Hallelujah! Praise be to God!"

THE RELIGIOUS COMMUNITIES

The West was a raw region, ripe for experimental living. Land on the frontier was cheap, so settlers could choose to live apart from the "corrupting" influence of other communities. For these reasons religious societies thrived on the old western frontier.

"Again a day is passed and a step made nearer to our end. Our time runs away and the joys of Heaven are our reward." These words were cried out each night by a minister in the town of Harmonie, Indiana. Harmonie was founded in 1815 by a religious leader named George Rapp.

Its first inhabitants were eight hundred German immigrants. Rapp told his followers that the world would soon end, so they must build a perfect town in the wilds of America and wait for God's final judgment. Rapp's flock lost faith when the world failed to end on his schedule.

Many other religious communities blossomed on the western frontier. Their members thought of them as utopias—ideal communities—where people worshiped God and strove to achieve perfection. The religious societies met with success as well as with disappointment.

A community of 20,000 Mormons lived in Nauvoo, Illinois. The Mormons were driven out of Illinois by neighbors who objected to their practice of polygamy. Polygamy allows a man to have more than one wife. After leaving Illinois, the Mormons established a thriving colony in Utah.

A sect called the Shakers moved from the eastern states and set up communities throughout the western frontier. They were called Shakers because their prayer sessions were so emotional that they caused members to shake with intensity. Shaker Heights, now a suburb of Cleveland, Ohio, was originally one of their settlements.

By and large the people who set up religious communities were gentle folk who tried to live a Christian life. An exception was a society headed by James Jesse Strang. Strang broke from the Mormon Church and organized his own religious community on Beaver Island in Lake Michigan. There, on an isolated island, Strang imagined himself a king. In fact, he crowned himself King James I. Those followers who dared question Strang's authority were tied to the village whipping post and flogged. Despite this brutal treatment Strang attracted more than five thousand men and women to his community. Finally he was shot and killed by two members of his congregation.

HEALING AND FAITH

Today it is difficult to imagine the terror felt by a frontier mother nursing her child through a fever. Doctors were few. Often doctors' treatments were ineffective. Worst of all, the mother with a sick child was haunted by

Quacks, or people pretending to be doctors,
sold useless potions to trusting pioneers.

memories of recent deaths: one of the twins down the road, her own nephew last year, the neighbor's little girl. Sicknesses and epidemics struck the frontier with grim regularity. And the diseases were most cruel to children.

ABRAHAM LINCOLN, SON OF THE WESTERN FRONTIER

Abraham Lincoln was born in Kentucky in 1809. He moved with his family to Indiana when he was seven, and later moved to Illinois. As a boy he had to help his father and mother run the family farm. For that reason he spent only about twelve months total in frontier schools. Still he became one of the most brilliant presidents in American history. Today much is made of the fact that Abraham Lincoln was born in a log cabin. But his log cabin childhood did not mean that Lincoln grew up poor. Log cabin communities in the West were the "working-class neighborhoods" of the time. Lincoln never thought of his family or his neighbors as being impoverished. The future president grew up under the same circumstances as did thousands of other boys and girls on the old western frontier.

Abraham Lincoln was no stranger to hard work. He earned his nickname the Railsplitter because of his skill with the ax.

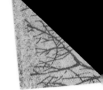

A pioneer family might have eight to ten children but see only five of them live to adulthood. Younger children were most likely to die from sicknesses. Some parents reported that they did not even want to know their children well until after they reached age six. Distancing oneself from a tiny child lessened the pain a parent felt if the child died.

Killer diseases common on the frontier included typhoid, tuberculosis, and smallpox. Everyone, young and old, feared cholera. A highly contagious disease, cholera swept through the western frontier in 1833 and again in 1839. Its victims were seized by vomiting and diarrhea. Many people suffering from cholera died after three to five agonizing days. A disease called milk sickness was common in Illinois and Indiana. The disease was probably caused by drinking milk from cows that had eaten poisonous weeds. In 1818 Nancy Lincoln, an Indiana pioneer, died of milk sickness. Mrs. Lincoln's death deeply saddened her nine-year-old son, Abraham.

People combated disease in various ways. Many pioneers tried to heal a sick relative through fervent prayer. Ministers were called to a sick person's home as frequently as were doctors. Settlers also bought bottles of medicine from roadside peddlers. Some had colorful names such as Merchants Celebrated Gargling Oil for Man and Beast. Popular among older people was Dr. Watson's Great Invincible Stiff Joint Panacea. The stiff joint medicine was advertised in these words: "Discovered along the Nile River, [it] has astonished every beholder."

Folk remedies and folk cures were popular on the western frontier. Some common practices, such as chewing on a chamomile plant to reduce toothache pain, were effective. A few methods of healing seem very strange today. It was believed that an onion carried in one's pocket would prevent snakebite. A dead spider put on a string around a child's neck would bring down his or her fever. A toad placed on a cut would diminish infection. Someone suffering epileptic seizures was advised to walk under the branches of a walnut tree three times. Most of these folk cures were brought from the East or from Europe. No one knows their origin or their degree of success. But the folk cures gave comfort and hope to desperately sick pioneers.

⇒ 5 ⇐

A Knack for Turning Work into Play

"An election in Kentucky lasts three days, and during that period whisky and apple toddy flow through the villages like [a river]."

—GEORGE PRENTICE, A JOURNALIST REPORTING
FOR AN EASTERN NEWSPAPER IN 1830

PARTIES FOR ALL OCCASIONS

George Prentice, the reporter who visited Kentucky at voting time, was astonished that a simple election would cause so much excitement and lead to such merriment. But on the western frontier just about any event was an excuse to throw a party. The pioneers had a genius for turning work into play.

Building a log cabin, for example, was fun as well as toil. The fun began with a log-rolling contest. Trees were felled and positioned as if on a starting line. At a signal a team of four or five men tried to roll its log to the cabin site faster than the other teams.

Log-rolling was a man's activity, but women too combined work with pleasure. Women organized spinning parties, quilting parties, and even chicken-and goose-plucking sessions. While working, the women chatted and sometimes sang a few songs.

POLITICS AND THE WEST

Because poor roads slowed communications, a voter who lived deep within the frontier had to wait up to two months to learn which candidate had won the presidential election. But this isolation did not dim the frontiersman's enthusiasm about politics. In 1828 Andrew Jackson was elected president, largely with the help of voters on the western frontier. Jackson had lived in frontier Tennessee. Westerners considered Jackson to be one of their own, so many pioneers traveled to Washington to give the new president a victory party. But the party soon got out of hand. Jackson supporters crowded into the White House, where they broke chairs and tore down curtains. Jackson had to flee his well-wishers by escaping through a White House window.

A husking bee was more than just work. It was a time to talk with old friends or a chance to meet a mate.

All pioneers joined in corn-husking parties. At such a party freshly picked corn was piled into several heaps. Teams then descended on the heaps, stripped the husks off the corn, and tossed the husked ears into a barrel. The first team to fill its barrel won. During the huskings hands flew fast. Young people giggled. A custom stated that a young man who happened to get a red ear of corn was allowed to kiss the girl to his right. The farmer who sponsored the party was rewarded by having all his corn husked in one day. The farmer, in turn, held a dance. An unnamed pioneer wrote a poem about corn-husking parties:

> *It was for all that, order of its kind,*
> *'Twas fun and useful industry combined.*

Weddings were a grand time of feast and frolic, even though the ceremony itself was simple. The bride was bound to be young. A pioneer girl who reached the age of twenty and was still unmarried was thought of as a spinster. Wedding feasts were usually held outside. The mother of the bride took days preparing the wedding dinner. She borrowed as many fancy dishes from neighbors as she could. A guest at an Indiana wedding wrote, "The table fairly reeled under the weight of roast beef, pork, and turkey, stacks of cakes and pies, with cornbread and wheat bread and homemade molasses—all plentifully interspersed with cabbage, beans, potatoes, baked custard, pickles, catsup, and pepper sauce."

Someone usually brought a fiddle to a wedding. After the guests stuffed themselves on the food, the fiddler held his instrument on his chest and began to "saw out a tune." Men, women, and children formed rings and performed different versions of the square dance. "Skip to My Lou, My Darling" was a favorite dance number. Settlers knew the words to dozens of familiar songs. They sang together as they danced: "Green grow the rushes, O! / Kiss her quick and let her go!" Many dancers "cut the double shuffle," meaning they leaped high in the air to the music. Always the dances were accompanied by clapping, the stamping of feet, and wild shouts of "Whoopee!"

SPORTS AND GAMES

Shooting matches were the most popular sport among pioneer men. Money as well as cows and pigs were bet on the outcome of shooting "bees." A common target was a square-inch piece of paper mounted on a roofing shingle. In uncanny displays of accuracy, frontier marksmen hit this tiny bull's-eye again and again from distances of seventy-five to one hundred yards.

Men also held horse races and footraces. They participated in strength contests, measuring who could throw a heavy rock the farthest. Wrestling matches drew large crowds. Frontier "rasslers" practiced grips such as the square hold, the side hold, and the Indian hug. Westerners enjoyed

Men were sent to bring home the Christmas turkey.
They turned it into a shooting match.

hunting even when their farms were well established and they no longer
needed wild game for food. The hunter's "hound dog" was his trusted and
loved assistant. Hounds that were skilled in chasing foxes became legends
in frontier communities.

Children created their own toys and devised their own games. Girls

With a simple knife, frontier boys played a game called mumblety-peg. The object was to flip the knife so the blade stuck in the ground. The loser had to pull a peg out of the dirt with his teeth.

fashioned dolls or toy animals out of yarn. Now and then a local wood-carver would whittle elegant dollhouse furniture out of wood and present the pieces to neighboring girls. Boys made sleds, wagons, and bows and arrows. Boys and girls sledded and ice-skated during the winter. The game Hide the Thimble amused small children when they were confined to the cabin on frigid winter evenings. Crack the Whip was played during school recess. Eight or ten children held hands to form the "whip." They ran like a spoke in a wheel until the child at the whip "handle" stopped. The sudden stop created a wave that sent the child at the whip's end tumbling.

Many log cabin communities were made up of extended families. This meant that grandparents lived under the same roof with the mother, father, and half a dozen or more children. Traditionally the grandmother was the storyteller of the family. On long winter nights children would beg Grandma to tell a favorite story, even though they had heard it dozens of times before.

Schools sponsored academic games such as spelling bees. Winners formed a team that competed against the best spellers of a neighboring school. Schools also promoted debating societies. Parents walked for miles to watch their children compete in spelling and debating contests. Eastern intellectuals sometimes denounced the people of the western frontier as being crude and uncultured. It was true that most adults lacked formal education. But the pioneers took enormous pride in their children's abilities to read, write, talk, and spell correctly.

THE FRONTIER CHARACTER

In the early 1830s an Englishwoman named Frances Trollope toured the United States. She wrote a book called *Domestic Manners of the Americans*. Mrs. Trollope was shocked by the uncouth manners she observed in the West: "The frightful manner of feeding with their knives, till the whole blade seemed to enter into the mouth; and the still more frightful manner of cleaning the teeth afterward with a pocket knife soon forced me to feel that I was not surrounded by [the gentlemen] of the Old World."

The western frontier, particularly in the early years, was a crude land. Roads were muddy. Few stores operated. Farms were unfenced. Pigs, chickens, and dogs foraged for food around the cabins. To travelers from the East, the people appeared crude also. Their homespun clothes, which were often hand-me-downs from friends or relatives, seemed to hang from their bodies. When people worked, their faces, hands, and clothes went unwashed. Adults and children walked barefoot in the warmer months. And the men had a self-destructive habit of getting drunk.

The West was a man's world. Fathers made the important decisions for the family. Community leaders such as preachers, schoolteachers, and politicians were almost always men. Women were not allowed to vote.

THE ERIE CANAL AND THE WESTERN FRONTIER

In 1825 construction on the Erie Canal was completed. The 363-mile-long canal ran the width of New York State and through the Appalachian Mountain chain. The new canal allowed immigrants to the West to travel

The canal boat **Seneca Chief** *opened the Erie Canal on October 25, 1825. Now even more settlers poured into the West, changing the face of the nation.*

by barge to the town of Buffalo on the shores of Lake Erie. From there farmers and workers took lake boats to western frontier ports such as Detroit, Chicago, and Cleveland. The Erie Canal changed settlement patterns. Before the canal was completed, Illinois and Indiana were being settled from the bottom up largely by southerners. The Erie Canal brought enormous numbers of northerners to the northern halves of those states. To this day, many people in southern Illinois and Indiana speak with southern accents while northern residents often have a flat midwestern twang.

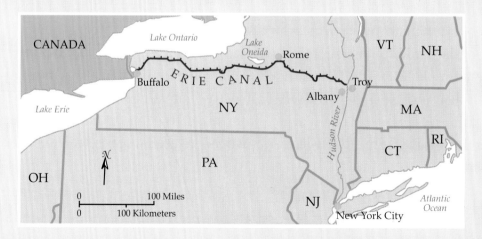

Corn liquor was scorned by the preachers, but most westerners thought drinking was a man's privilege. More often it was a vice. Whisky made from corn had a nasty taste. Just half a jug made a man falling-down drunk. The liquor was sold by log cabin distillers who gave their product various names, including Racehorse, Moral Suasion, and Pig and Whistle. Men attended parties, jug in hand. Fights broke out. No gentlemanly rules of combat held sway during a drunken frontier brawl. Strangling and eye gouging were common tactics. Travelers commented on how often they saw a frontiersman missing an earlobe. The lobe had been bitten off during a fight.

Churches and schools helped to civilize the West. So did the arrival of more people from the East. As communities expanded, the people's commitment to law and order grew also. Courts and sheriff's offices were established. Men who were habitual drunkards or bullies were put in jail. Murderers, cattle rustlers, and horse thieves were hanged.

Despite widespread drunkenness most people were safe from crime in the West. A sober and sensible man could avoid fights simply by shunning the company of men who were passing a jug at a party. Roads were safe for travelers. Robbery hardly existed. And an astounding degree of friendliness prevailed among the pioneers. Most log cabins had a latch-string poking through a hole in their doors. A visitor need only pull on the latch-string to lift the inside latch and enter the home. A common expression was, "Our latch-string is always out." The saying meant that visitors were always welcome.

✦6✦
The Frontier Moves West

*"Old America seems to be breaking up and
moving westward. We are seldom out of sight,
as we travel toward the Ohio [River],
of family groups behind and before us."*

—MORRIS BIRKBECK, A WESTWARD TRAVELER,
WRITING IN 1817

ENDING THE INDIAN CONFLICT

Above the door of every pioneer cabin was a rifle rack, often made of deer's antlers. There the father's rifle lay, always within an easy grasp. For the early settlers a rifle was key to life itself. The first pioneers in the western frontier lived in constant fear of Indian raids. Attacks against a single cabin usually came at dawn. Ten to twenty warriors, armed with tomahawks and rifles, surrounded the cabin and rushed it from all sides. The Native Americans shrieked frightening war whoops and battle cries as they charged. Every man and boy within the cabin fired from the windows or from specially built gun ports. Women and girls stood behind, reloading the rifles.

Defending their lands from the rush
of western settlers, Indians fought back.

Sometimes the raiders were content to run away with the family's horses and cattle. But warriors often killed entire households, sparing only the teenagers. Teenage boys and girls were taken prisoner and either held for ransom or incorporated into the tribe. Jemima Boone, the fourteen-year-old daughter of Daniel Boone, was captured by Indians while she was out canoeing with friends. As the kidnappers took Jemima to their camp she secretly attached tiny pieces of her dress to trees. Her father was able to follow the trail and rescue her. Jemima Boone's cool thinking in the face of danger made her a hero on the old western frontier. In later years grandmothers told Jemima's story over and over again to enchanted children.

The settlers' best defense was to spot a raiding party before it attacked. Farmers kept a keen eye on the woods as they worked. The pioneers relied on their dogs to warn them of approaching strangers. Settlers who saw hostile warriors alerted neighboring cabins at once. A fast runner or horseman was chosen to spread the alarm. Given time, the settlers retreated to a stockade. Stockades were log forts usually built near rivers. Rarely was an Indian band large enough to storm a heavily defended stockade and overcome the settlers within.

On occasion the Native Americans and the pioneers tried to be friendly with one another. Sometimes they traded goods. But generally hatred prevailed between the two groups. The Indians regarded the pioneers as invaders of their land. The pioneers thought of the Indians as less than human.

The Indians had no chance to drive back the flood of settlers moving onto the western frontier. Their forces suffered a major defeat in the Battle of Tippecanoe, fought in 1811 near present-day Lafayette, Indiana. The British defeat in the War of 1812 also hurt the Indian cause. The British had been arming Indians in the western frontier and urging them to fight the American settlers.

By the 1830s the Indians were no longer a threat on the western frontier, although small wars and skirmishes still broke out. For thousands of years Native Americans had lived, hunted, and farmed in the forests west of the Appalachians. Now, faced with the onslaught of settlers, most were forced

TECUMSEH, MAN OF VISION

The western frontier was home to many different tribes: the Miami, the Potawatomi, the Shawnee, and others. Before the arrival of settlers these groups had been bitter rivals. One Shawnee chief, Tecumseh, urged the tribes to forget their past differences. He told the Indian nations to stand up as one people and resist the pioneer invasion. Tecumseh, who was born in Ohio, was a brilliant speaker. Yet even he was unable to unite the Indian peoples. During the War of 1812 he joined British forces in hopes of stemming the American advance into western lands. He was killed in battle in 1813. Today Tecumseh is an American legend. His name comes from a Shawnee word meaning "shooting star."

to move west of the Mississippi. And in the years to come they had to move again as America expanded toward the Pacific.

INDUSTRIES TRANSFORM THE FRONTIER

Mills for grinding corn were among the first industries to operate on the western frontier. Mills were built near rivers. Flowing river currents turned a waterwheel, which in turn drove great stone grinding wheels. The stones crushed the corn into meal. People walked or rode on horseback carrying sacks of corn to the mill. Previously they had ground corn into meal by the laborious process of putting the kernels on a tree stump and pounding them with a log. The opening of a mill was always greeted with enthusiasm in the community.

Many farmers on the old western frontier had no cash. However, the mill operator could be persuaded to grind corn in exchange for a few chickens or a calf. Storekeepers frequently set up shop near mills. The storekeepers reasoned that settlers might buy or trade for goods while they waited for their corn to be ground. Thus industries and shops encouraged the growth of tiny towns.

Sawmills soon opened. The sawmills had huge circular saws, which were also operated by waterwheels driven by river currents. The mills took in raw logs and turned out finished boards. Nails finally became available in western stores. Nails were made in the East by workers who cut them out of a thin bar of iron. They had square shanks that tapered down to a point. The availability of boards and nails allowed a farm family to build a frame house. Yet most farmers still used their old log cabins to store tools or to house chickens or pigs. Some of the sturdy log cabins stood on farm sites for more than one hundred years.

Improved roads brought still more people to the western frontier. The Wilderness Road led through the Appalachians and into Kentucky and Tennessee. To the north

Mills sprang up on the swift-moving rivers of the frontier. What had once taken days to grind could now be done in hours. Industry had come to the frontier.

the National Road (also called the Cumberland Road) led five hundred miles from Cumberland, Maryland, to Vandalia, Illinois. Although the roads were lengthened, they were still just dirt. In muddy sections they were often paved with split logs. The logs were placed with the flat sides up. These log sections were called corduroy roads. They made for a bumpy ride, but they allowed the passage of horse-drawn wagons.

In 1811 a steamboat left from Pennsylvania, chugged along the Ohio River to the Mississippi, and then steamed south to New Orleans. That

Once a vast wilderness, steamboats and streetlamps
had arrived in the Ohio River valley.

1811 trip was America's first long voyage by a river steamboat. Soon paddle-wheel steamboats ran a regular service on the Ohio. The vessels brought people and goods westward far more efficiently than the old flatboats.

By 1854 a railroad line reached the Mississippi River at Rock Island, Illinois. At the time the railroad was completed older Americans could remember when George Washington was president and the western frontier was a vast forest. To them a railroad linking the Atlantic coast with the Mississippi seemed miraculous.

A FRONTIER NO MORE

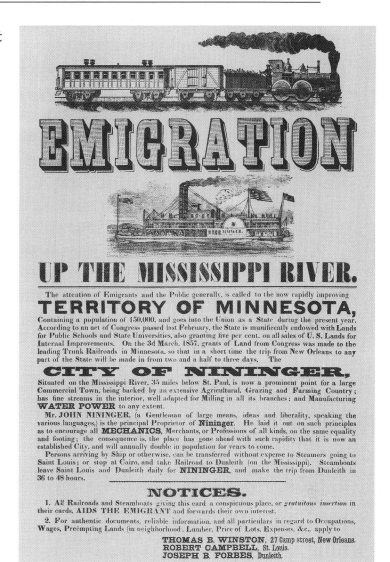

Advertisements promising a better life lured settlers west

Cheap and fertile land acted as a magnet drawing farm families to the West. Farmers in the eastern states abandoned the rocky soil of Vermont and New Hampshire and marched westward to till the rich black earth of Ohio and Indiana. So many farm families were drawn to the West that a New England newspaper raised the alarm: "[There are] plots to drain the east of its best blood."

Settlers also flooded in from Ireland, England, France, Germany,

FROM TERRITORIES TO STATES

Anticipating the nation's western expansion, Congress made laws governing the admission of new states to the American Union. When a region had sufficient population (usually 60,000 people) it could apply for statehood. Kentucky was admitted in 1792 as the fifteenth American state and the first state in the old western frontier. Tennessee was admitted in 1796 as the sixteenth state.

Norway, Sweden, Finland, and Denmark. Farmland was expensive in overcrowded Europe. European peasants looked upon cheap land in the New World as a gift from God. Many Europeans skipped over the eastern states and headed directly for the West. A New York journalist who boarded a crowded steamboat on the Ohio River in 1833 claimed he heard "half as many languages as were spoken at Babel."

Cities developed at river and lake ports. Cleveland, on Lake Erie, was founded in 1796 by a land speculator named Moses Cleaveland. From the beginning Cleaveland looked upon the new town as his namesake. But, according to one story, an editor in one of the town's first newspapers misspelled his name, and it has been "Cleveland" ever since. Chicago began as an Indian fur-trading post on the shores of Lake Michigan. Its founder was a black man named Jean Baptiste Pointe du Sable. No city in history expanded as fast as Chicago. In just fifty years it grew from a muddy village to the second-largest city in the country.

The vast lands north of the Ohio River were known as the Northwest Territory (established in 1787). As settlers flocked in, the area was subdivided into various territories. Eventually states were formed:

Ohio in 1803, Indiana in 1816, Illinois in 1818, Michigan in 1837, and Wisconsin in 1848.

The great swell in population and the rise of cities meant that the land between the Appalachian Mountains and the Mississippi River was a frontier no more. By 1840 Americans considered this region to be an established and stable part of their country.

Even though the land was settled, Americans never forgot the spirit of the pioneers who ventured into the western forests. The pioneers' poems, stories, and songs are celebrated even today. One song loved by pioneers was "El-a-noy," named for a mispronunciation of Illinois. It is a song praising the rich and fruitful land of the West. Pioneers especially enjoyed belting out the chorus:

> *Way down upon the Wabash*
> *Such land was never known.*
> *If Adam had passed over it,*
> *The soil he'd surely own;*
> *He'd think it was the garden*
> *He played in when a boy,*
> *And straight pronounce it Eden*
> *In the State of El-a-noy.*
> ***Chorus:***
> *Then move your family westward;*
> *Good health you will enjoy,*
> *And rise to wealth and honor*
> *In the State of El-a-Noy.*

Glossary

board: Regular meals provided for a lodger.

cede: To give away, or to give up land.

concept: Idea or notion.

conservationist: One who wishes to preserve natural resources.

convulsive: Having to do with violent, involuntary motions.

corduroy roads: Roads that are paved with logs at the muddy spots to ease the passage of wagons.

denounce: To condemn; to disagree sharply with a suggestion.

epidemic: An uncontrolled spreading of a disease.

exhortation: Advice given in a strong and urgent way.

flatboat: Any kind of boat (including crude log rafts) with a flat bottom, designed to float down rivers.

habitual: Usual, customary.

inaugurate: To make a formal beginning.

invariably: Always.

ironic: A surprising twist from the expected.

laborious: Difficult, with much labor.

luster: Brilliant shine.

mystic: A person who seemingly has supernatural powers.

onslaught: A sudden attack.

panacea: A remedy for all problems or difficulties; a cure-all.

penning: Keeping people in a certain area.

prevail: To persist or continue.

recitation: Phrases repeated from memory.

reel: To walk or move unsteadily.

rent: Tore or ripped.

spinster: An older, unmarried woman.

squatter: A person who settled down and farmed a piece of land without paying for it.

switch: A slender stick used to punish a person.

trek: To hike; to journey.

uncouth: Loud or offensive.

utopia: An ideal community.

whittle: To carve wood with a knife.

The Old Western Frontier

PART OF MINNESOTA

LAKE SUPERIOR

MICHIGAN

LAKE HURON

WISCONSIN
1848

Grayling

Ludington

LAKE MICHIGAN

MICHIGAN
1837

Mount Horeb

Detroit

Chicago

Tippecanoe River

Cleveland

Pittsburgh

ME
1820

VT
1791

NH

NY

MA

CT RI

Erie Canal

LAKE ONTARIO

PA

LAKE ERIE

Rock Island

ILLINOIS
1818

Lafayette

OHIO
1805

Marietta

National Road

NJ

MD

DE

Nauvoo

Springfield

INDIANA
1816

Cincinnati

Ohio River

New Salem

Vandalia

New Harmony

Boonesborough

VA

ATLANTIC
OCEAN

APPALACHIAN MOUNTAINS

Danville

Wilderness Road

KENTUCKY
1792

Cumberland Gap

Johnson City

NC

Nashville

TENNESSEE
1796

Mississippi River

SC

GA

New Orleans

The Old Western Frontier

0   500km

0   300 mi

N

The Old Western Frontier in Time

1750—An American explorer named Thomas Walker follows an old Indian trail and discovers the Cumberland Gap, a natural passage through the Appalachian Mountains; the Cumberland Gap later becomes the gateway to the southern portion of the old western frontier.

1775—Daniel Boone leads a party of settlers through the Cumberland Gap; Boone blazes a trail called the Wilderness Road into the wilds of what are now Kentucky and Tennessee.

1783—The United States gains its independence from Great Britain; the British cede the lands west of the Appalachian Mountains to the young American nation; the territory between the Appalachians and the Mississippi River becomes America's western frontier.

1787—Congress passes the Northwest Ordinance, which lays the groundwork for government on the western frontier; the ordinance forbids slavery in the region north of the Ohio River, guarantees freedom of religion for all settlers, and encourages education.

1788—More than one thousand wooden rafts and flatboats carrying farm families stream down the Ohio River heading for the western frontier.

1792—Kentucky becomes the fifteenth American state; it is the first state west of the Appalachians.

1796—Tennessee is admitted as the sixteenth American state.

1803—Ohio enters the Union as the seventeenth American state.

1808—Tecumseh, Shawnee chief, tries to unite Native American nations from the Great Lakes to Florida.

1811—Work begins on the National Road (also called the Cumberland Road), which will eventually link Maryland with Illinois.

1811—William Henry Harrison, governor of the Indiana Territory, leads troops in a major battle against Indian forces at the Tippecanoe River, the Native Americans are defeated.

1812—The War of 1812, between Great Britain and the United States, begins; Britain is forced to stop supplying western Indians with arms.

1816—Indiana enters the Union as the nineteenth state.

1818—Illinois enters the Union as America's twenty-first state.

1825—The Erie Canal is completed in New York State; immigrants to the West can now travel by barge on the canal to the city of Buffalo on Lake Erie, from there, they can go by ship through the Great Lakes to western frontier ports.

1828—Andrew Jackson is elected president; Jackson, from Tennessee, gains his office largely because of his popularity with voters in the West.

1833—A deadly epidemic of cholera sweeps through the West, killing hundreds of settlers.

1837—Chicago, with a population of about four thousand, is incorporated as a city; it soon becomes the second-largest city in the nation.

1837—Michigan becomes the twenty-sixth state.

1848—Wisconsin enters the Union as the thirtieth state; it is the last territory in the old western frontier to achieve statehood.

Places to Visit

ILLINOIS

Chicago:

The Chicago Historical Society displays models of Fort Dearborn, a stockade that was destroyed by Indians in 1812. Other models show how Chicago looked when it was a frontier village. The museum also holds a wealth of Lincoln material, including an oxen yoke that Lincoln carved when he was a young man on the Illinois frontier.

Nauvoo:

In 1838 about 15,000 Mormons established the settlement of Nauvoo, along the Mississippi River in central Illinois. It was one of many religious communities that blossomed on the old western frontier. The Mormons were disliked by their neighbors because their religion allowed a man to have more than one wife. In 1844, amid growing hostility, the Mormons fled Nauvoo. They moved west and founded Salt Lake City in Utah. Visitors to Nauvoo today can see the restored homes of Brigham Young and Joseph Smith, two important Mormon leaders. There are also the ruins of the Mormon Temple.

Springfield:

New Salem Village (near Springfield) is an authentic reproduction of the log cabin community where young Abraham Lincoln lived from 1831 to 1837. The reproductions include the Lincoln-Berry General Store, of which he was part owner. Visitors also enter the log post office where the future president served as postmaster.

INDIANA

Lafayette:

Visitors walk the grounds of the Tippecanoe Battlefield, the site of the 1811 battle that proved to be a costly defeat for the region's Indians. Mementos of the battle are displayed at the Tippecanoe County Historical Museum. The commanding general at Tippecanoe was William Henry Harrison. He later used the fame earned by his victory to be elected president in 1840. His vice presidential running mate was John Tyler. During the campaign Harrison's followers chanted the catchy slogan "Tippecanoe and Tyler too!"

New Harmony:
Here lies a beautifully restored village that was once one of the many "utopias" on the western frontier. New Harmony is the second incarnation of the religious community of Harmonie, first founded by George Rapp and his German followers. In 1825 Rapp sold the village to Robert Owen. Owen established a socialist colony he called New Harmony. Both social experiments failed within ten years. Visitors at New Harmony today tour interesting sites such as a frontier doctor's office and a concert hall.

KENTUCKY
Cumberland Gap National Historic Park:
Here rises the natural pass first used by the explorer Thomas Walker in 1750. Twenty-five years later Daniel Boone made his famous journey through the pass. Beyond the Cumberland Gap lay the Wilderness Road over which 200,000 pioneers ventured into the southern portion of the western frontier. Seventy miles of hiking trails in this park allow visitors to relive the adventure of early western frontier settlers.

Danville:
In 1792 the constitution for the new state of Kentucky was adopted in Danville's Constitution Square. Visitors today get a feel for pioneer life by touring a restored log cabin, church, courthouse, and jail. Nearby is the Pioneer Playhouse in Village-of-the-Arts, a reproduction of an eighteenth-century Kentucky village.

MICHIGAN
Grayling:
Hartwick Pines State Park contains Michigan's only large grove of virgin trees. Hiking through this towering pine forest gives visitors an idea of the woodlands that greeted the pioneers of the old western frontier. An interpretive center in the park tells the story of the stately white pine trees that once covered this region of Michigan.

Ludington:
White Pine Village is a re-created log cabin community of the early 1800s. Included are the general store, the courthouse, the jail, and a one-room schoolhouse.

OHIO
Marietta:
Marietta (founded in 1788) was the first permanent village in the Northwest Territory. Today the Campus Martius Museum preserves several log buildings, including the house of Rufus Putnam, Marietta's founder. Exhibits at the nearby Ohio River Museum show the development of river craft, including examples of flatboats that once carried the pioneers west.

Schoenbrunn Village:
Missionaries, hoping to convert Indians to Christianity, built a settlement here in 1772. In the Schoenbrunn Village stands what is believed to be Ohio's first schoolhouse. Nearby is the Fort Laurens State Memorial, a re-creation of a defensive stockade.

TENNESSEE

Johnson City:

At the Rocky Mount Historical Site stands an authentically re-created log cabin. Inside are fine examples of pioneer furniture. Visitors can take a two-hour tour and watch costumed staff members re-create a typical day in the life of a pioneer family. Also on the grounds are examples of a barn, a blacksmith's shop, and a slave cabin. The slave cabin is a sad reminder that slavery was allowed in the southern part of the old western frontier.

Nashville:

About ten miles east of Nashville is the Hermitage, the home of Andrew Jackson, the seventh president of the United States. Jackson, like Lincoln, was born in a log cabin. The Hermitage is a stately mansion he built in 1819 and rebuilt in 1835. The fact that this elegant house could be constructed demonstrates the rapid progress achieved in frontier Tennessee.

WISCONSIN

Eagle:

Old World Wisconsin is a fascinating collection of pioneer buildings that were taken from various sites in the state and reassembled at this sprawling outdoor museum. Authentic barns, stores, churches, and even outhouses stand here. Volunteers dressed in pioneer clothing weave flax into yarn, make horseshoes, and perform other daily tasks.

Mount Horeb:

Wisconsin was settled by thousands of emigrants from northern Europe. They formed Finnish villages, Danish villages, German villages, and so on. At Mount Horeb is Little Norway, originally built in the 1850s. The village shows homes and furnishings fashioned by Norwegian settlers.

To Learn More...

BOOKS

Anderson, Joan W. Pioneer *Children of Appalachia*. New York: Clarion Books, 1990.

Andrist, Ralph K. *Steamboats on the Mississippi*. New York: American Heritage Books, 1962.

Barr, Roger. *The American Frontier*. San Diego: Lucent Books, 1996.

Chambers, Catherine E. *Flatboats on the Ohio: Westward Bound*. Mahwah, NJ: Troll Associates, 1984 (fiction).

————. *Frontier Village: A Town Is Born*. Mahwah, NJ: Troll Associates, 1984 (fiction).

Cobb, Mary. *The Quilt-Block History of Pioneer Days: With Projects Kids Can Make*. Brookfield, CT: Millbrook Press, 1995.

Hook, Jason. *Tecumseh: Visionary Chief of the Shawnee*. New York: Sterling Publishing,1989.

Lawlor, Laurie. *Daniel Boone*. Niles, IL: Albert Whitman, 1989.

Laycock, George, and Ellen Laycock. *How the Settlers Lived*. New York: David McKay Company, 1980.

Steele, William O. *The Old Wilderness Road: An American Journey*. New York: Harcourt Brace, 1968.

Steffof, Rebecca. *Women Pioneers*. New York: Facts on File, 1995.

Stowe, Harriet Beecher. *Uncle Tom's Cabin*. New York: Airmont, 1967 (fiction).

Tunis, Edwin. *Frontier Living*. New York: Harper Collins, 1976.

Wilder, Laura Ingalls. *Little House on the Prairie*. New York: Harper Collins, 1961.

AUDIO

Frontier Ballads, sung by Pete Seeger. On disc, in two parts: *The Trek, 1791–1814* and *The Settlers, 1814–1836*. Folkways Records, New York, 1954.

Half House, Half Alligator, stories of flatboat crews. Audiocassette, 65 minutes. August House Audio, Little Rock, AR, 1997.

Uncle Tom's Cabin, the Harriet Beecher Stowe classic on audiocassette (20 hours). Brilliance Corporation, Grand Haven, MI, 1998.

WEBSITES*

http://www.ohiohistory.org/kids/games/ history.html. The Ohio Historical Society Kids Pages is an interactive site that allows kids to write about various aspects of Ohio history (including the western frontier era) and then displays the best letters.

http://www.museum.state.il.us/exhibits/ athome/index.html. A site called "At Home in the Heartland online" encourages kids to click on various periods of Illinois history.

Websites change from time to time. For additional on-line information, check with the media specialist at your local library.

Bibliography

Andrist, Ralph K., ed. *The American Heritage History of the Making of the Nation*. New York: American Heritage Books, 1987.

Buley, R. Carlyle. *The Old Northwest, Pioneer Period, 1815-1840*. Vol. 1. Bloomington, IN: Indiana University Press, 1950.

Commager, Henry Steele, ed. *Witness to America: A Documentary History of the United States from its Discovery to Modern Times*. New York: Barnes & Noble Books, 1996.

Gabriel, Ralph Henry. *The Lure of the Frontier: A Story of Race Conflict*. New Haven, CT: Yale University Press, 1929.

Havighurst, Walter. *The Heartland: Ohio, Indiana, Illinois*. New York: Harper & Row, 1962.

Ketchum, Richard. *The American Heritage Book of the Pioneer Spirit*. New York: Simon & Schuster, 1959.

Madison, James H. *The Indiana Way*. Bloomington, IN: Indiana University Press, 1986.

McLaughlin, Robert. *The Heartland: Illinois, Indiana, Michigan, Ohio, Wisconsin*. New York: Time/Life Books, 1967.

Ogg, Frederic Austin. *The Old Northwest*. New Haven, CT: Yale University Press, 1919.

Rae, Noel, ed. *Witnessing America*. New York: Penguin Books, 1996.

The WPA Guide to Illinois. New York: Pantheon Books, 1983.

Notes on Quotes

The quotations in this book are from the following sources:

A Young Nation Looks Westwards
Page 7, "I am listening": Ketchum, *The American Heritage Book of the Pioneer Spirit*, p. 129.

Taming a Rugged Land
Page 11, "I was struck with astonishment": Andrist, *The American Heritage History of the Making of the Nation*, p. 162.

Page 13, "On ascending the riverbank": *The American Heritage History of the Making of the Nation*, p. 164.

Page 17, "An *ax* is their tool": Havighurst, *The Heartland*, p. 119.

Page 19, "Boys of twelve hung their heads": Ogg, *The Old Northwest*, p. 121.

Page 19, "I'll sing you a song": Havighurst, *The Heartland*, p. 112.

Life on the Log Cabin Frontier
Page 21, "A pair of good horses": *The WPA Guide to Illinois*, p. 27.

Page 23, "at once inexpressibly cold": McLaughlin, *The Heartland*, p. 33.

Page 27, "My mother used to spin": Commager, *Witness to America*, p. 282.

A People of Faith
Page 31, "A new exercise broke out": Rae, *Witnessing America*, p. 393.

Page 35, "The preachers became": Ogg, *The Old Northwest*, p. 127.

Page 35, "struck out right and left": Madison, *The Indiana Way*, p. 101.

Page 35, "Again a day is passed": McLaughlin, *The Heartland*, p. 54.

Page 39, "Discovered along the Nile": Buley, *The Old Northwest*, p. 305.

A Knack of Turning Work into Play
Page 41, "An election in Kentucky": *Witnessing America*, p. 311.

Page 43, "It was for all that": *The Old Northwest, Pioneer Period, 1815–1840*, p. 323.

Page 44, "The table fairly": *The Old Northwest*, p. 330.

Page 47, "The frightful manner of": *The American Heritage History of the Making of the Nation*, p. 174.

The Frontier Moves West
Page 51, "Old America seems": *Witness to America*, p. 259.

Page 57, "plots to drain": *The Old Northwest*, p. 98.

Page 58, "half as many languages": McLaughlin, *The Heartland*, p. 162.

Page 59, "Way down upon the Wabash": McLaughlin, *The Heartland*, p. 128.

Index

About the Author

Conrad Stein was born and grew up in Chicago. After serving in the United States Marines, he attended the University of Illinois and graduated with a degree in history. Mr. Stein is a full-time writer of books for young readers, with more than eighty titles published. He has traveled extensively in the Midwest and has seen much of the land that comprised the old western frontier.

Mr. Stein lives in Chicago with his wife, children's book author Deborah Kent, and their daughter, Janna.